Two Bowls of Joy

A Collection of 50 Poems

Danie Botha

Copyright © 2019
Danie Botha
Two Bowls of Joy
A Collection of 50 Poems
All rights reserved.

No part of this publication may be reproduced, distributed, or transmitted in any form or by any means, including photocopying, recording, or other electronic or mechanical methods, without the prior written permission of the publisher, except in the case of brief quotations embodied in critical reviews and certain other non-commercial uses permitted by copyright law.

Danie Botha
Published Under Charbellini Press
https://daniebotha.com

Printed in the United States of America
First Printing 2019
First Edition 2019
ISBN-13: 978-1-9994620-1-7

10 9 8 7 6 5 4 3 2 1

For Isaac, Aramis and Xeniya.
You too, are our joy!

I'll tell you how the sun rose—
a ribbon at a time.
The steeples swam in amethyst,
the news like squirrels ran.

The hills untied their bonnets,
the bobolinks begun.
Then I said softly to myself,
"That must have been the sun!"

Emily Dickinson, A Day.

A Collection Of 50 Poems
In Five Parts:
Life, Love, Loss,
Longing, & Laughter

Table of Contents

Author's Note 1

Part 1: Life 3

Mid-summer's Forest 4

The Five-fifteen 7

Smile, We're Strangers 8

African Interior 10

Color Within the Lines 11

In Pursuit of Healing 15

Anatomy Hall 19

Remedy 20

Resilience 23

Snow Paths 24

Part 2: Love 27

Cradle 28

Calling of a Scribe 31

Bosom Bared 33

Skin 35

Blackbird 37

Love that Lingers 39

Two Figures Dancing 40

Mended 41
I Should Have Loved You More 42
Prayer Without End 45

Part 3: Loss 47
What Stays Behind 48
Rachel, Weeping 49
Greetings and Goodbyes 53
Thirst 55
Twelve baskets 57
Hands 59
Footpaths 61
Voetpadlangs 64
In Memoriam: Father 67
Measuring a life 69

Part 4: Longing 71
Wonder 72
May You 73
Cormorant 75
Be Still 76
Last Week's Embrace 77
Brother 78
Enough 79

No Slaves to Yesterdays 80
I Will Rise.. 83
What's in Your Hand? 87

Part 5: Laughter & Joy 89
Two Bowls of Joy 90
Joy Comes in the Morning 91
Silly Poem 92
Slice of Sun 93
Traffic Light Troubadour 94
Beach Day (at the Lake).. 95
Morning 98
To Joy be Drawn... 99
Moonlit Beaches.. 101
Gift... 103

Thank you for reading! *105*
Also by Danie Botha... *107*

Author's Note

Poetry writing came to me only later in my life, years after I started writing and publishing my novels. Writing long-form fiction, in the beginning helped ground me, it became a channel to pour my soul into—writing has saved my life on more than one occasion. Writing helped me heal. Two years ago, amid profound personal loss and dramatic work-related stress, I discovered, through trial and error, how writing short-form fiction and poetry brought relief from mental anguish much faster than long-form fiction ever could.

The discipline of brevity, meter, metaphor, rhythm, and rhyme, forced me to delve deeper faster into the recesses of the soul and heart and mind to find clarity and meaning and healing. The original title for this debut poetry collection was, *What Stays Behind*, (Part 3: # 21), written weeks after Mother's passing in 2017. *Two Bowls of Joy (Part 5: #41)*, the present title, was written in the Summer of 2019. In a way, *Two Bowls of Joy* holds hands with *What Stays Behind*. It refers to the two measures (overs) of manna the people of Israel could pick up from the desert floor on the day before the Sabbath on their journey to the Promised Land, Canaan.

Reading Mike Mason's book, *Champagne for the Soul*, impacted me in profound ways. It helped me reappreciate the essence of joy and living and how big a part choice plays in it. Each day, each morning, we have to choose joy anew, as if for the first time. Each day, joy is possible, impossible as it may seem. Joy is inseparable from sorrow and pain—in the latter the former finds its footing. Pain and struggle and hardship in life is a given—for some more than others. Misery and joy are both optional—we choose one or the other. In our broken and dark and suffering world there is so much beauty and hope and wonder that we can do no less than leap and sing with joy, even if we wipe away a tear.

A bowl of joy to you!

Danie Botha

Winnipeg

18 October 2019

Part 1: Life

"The fear of death follows
from the fear of life.
A man who lives fully
is prepared to die
at any time."

Mark Twain

Mid-summer's Forest

Mosaic of shade and light
pave twisting path in colors slight

summer's green with trunks all black
heavenwards; some stooped, some trodden
bur oak and a paper birch, jack
pine, the aspen not forgotten.

Across the whitened winding way
industrious squirrel darts with zest
collecting nuts, a friend to play
robins calling from up high a nest

where snaking river sluggish flow,
earth-brown, midst the rustling reeds;
seeking sun, three snapping turtles show,
give chase, a dragonfly that feeds.

This late at day the heedful deer
takes refuge in the thicket, holds
back her fawn, whose prancing cheer,
white-tailed, gallant, until mother scolds.

The midday sun beats down upon
the naked heads and hikers' legs;
as forest breathes, the heat turns on;
discomfort irks! In search of robin eggs

a hawk appears, returns where matted feathers
lay, his regal beak affirms: I am the bird of prey.
Spider's web from wind in tethers,
whisp'ring breeze gives birth—a song so gay.

Listen, do! All trav'lers make a choice: hear
mellow music flow, rip each and ev'ry leave—
invigorates, elates; gusto does the soul now steer
as velvet forest floor with moss does weave

mosaic of shade and light
when comes the morn', has dropped from sight

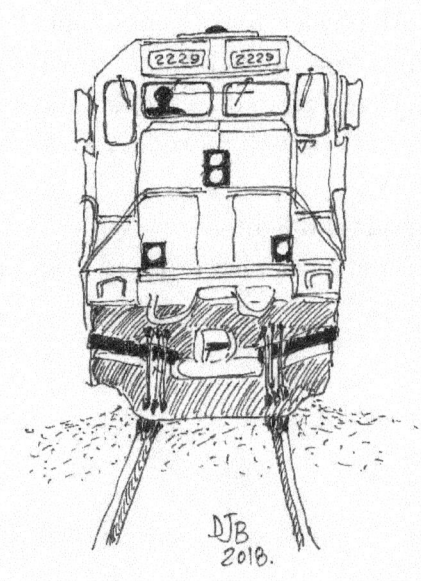

The Five-fifteen

Defying logic,
disobeying physics'
laws, a chance encounter
on the five-fifteen—hissing
doors at Knightsbridge station
where shuttled sheep do huddle:
hundred harried faces, eyes glued
to hand-held devices. A presence felt,
imaginary shake of hands; furtive glance,
knotted brow, as hint of rouge ascends,
pleads ignorance. Doors slide open, then
hiss closed: South Kensington station. When
Earl's Court flashes past, a second glance
deemed necessary—how brazen now
we are. Sans protocol: unwavering
the stare, a dimple in her cheek,
a mole below her ear, the
shadow of a smile—she
sensed my hesitation.
I missed my stop at
Parson's Green! A
chance encounter
on the five-fifteen.

Smile, We're Strangers

Elbowed antennae in a quiver
workers scurry in pinstripe pantsuits

on their way to feed the queen.

Between Brooklyn and the Bronx
they lose the trail of pheromones

misplace the map to Down- and Uptown—

how harried is the hurried;
do listen up you fools: get out my way

don't talk don't touch

don't dare to stare
at the middle of the universe,

or piercings in my nose—

you'll always find a yellow door
(it used to be the yellow pages),

the key to which on velvet floor

beside the street musician's open case;
all stairwells lead to Queens

get out my way I said

and shift your chair with wheels
how dare you smile we're strangers!

your slanted legs demand

a frown as crown
how dare you rub your

joy your happiness

across my furrowed brow
I'm on my way to feed the queen.

African Interior

single-file the children trudged downhill
with hat in hand instructed to be quiet
past bougainvillea red and lavender latticed

into trees long before cicadas woke—drowning
out all happy banter when they do (such silly
stipulation!)—with teacher at the door

in broad-rim hat five-and-twenty all in all
grades one through seven blessed with blackboards
wall to wall a bell of brass to mute the class

a prayer and a song some mental math
go out and play while Miss instructs the
older kids—to read and write without a smite

the final bell—the midday meal with sun
out high makes teacher sigh stands at the door
inspects each head—points at the sky

now heed the sun she preaches, (tucks a
hat all straight) stick to shade you do not
play with sunstroke mind the rattlesnakes

do not doodle less you wish for *Housemom's*
madness—single-file the children strolled uphill
singing shouting louder than cicadas in the African
Interior

Color Within the Lines

Having paid attention in Kindergarten paid off as I grapple
with what colour best to paint my lips and hide my unclothed
(famished) soul a teaspoon sun a pinch of moon and get it
inside out and upside down in rainbow flavours stay within
the lines and listen to the news

no one does that any more

are you serious you're not on Sirius only cable it's a shame a circus
and the moisturizer stretched between two quarter poles slanted
for the proper pitch of roof allowing the trapeze to tumble like a
clown who coloured outside the broken yellow line that indicates
a lane and we're all in agreement

that we disagree on what art is

and the folly of the critique and the gatekeeper and the subjectivity
of what constitutes literary and literacy and a litany of larceny
provided it is done with taste adhering to the dress-code for a black-tie
event shining with sophistication looking down fresh nose jobs
(a revision non the less)

that has lost its sense of smell

and propriety and brim with pride and prejudice applauding famous couples drinking whole leaf green tea casting shadows while regaling reckless reporters with breaking news about their latest breakup binging on leather sofas stuffing faces with crisps and dips and sauces with lips laced with filler

resembling roll up rims of coffee cups

the latest craze in fatty-tires covering the dark spots with foundation and blusher don't forget the Q-tip, rules are rules for a reason demonstrating ignorance insofar approaching royalty with caution if not infamy.

In Pursuit of Healing

Hippocrates was a healer not a hypocrite a Greek from Kos teaching illness stemmed from ailments not divine

inflictions doled as punishment advising 'gainst healing

people unwilling giving up what made them ill at the center of modern medicine we pay mere lip-service to his

Oath while turning our profession into business making

loads of money for a handful limiting access to the privileged and the patient (those not dead we'll see you

in a year) making lists of neologisms, fancy words for

obscure ailment and disease design a pill and powder for each one or fabricate a brand-new name for maladies to

fit the drugs we've dreamed up in a lab the goose with

golden eggs while mentors from the past taught first to do no harm *primum non nocere* we laugh at such

outdated pearls of wisdom getting writer's cramp so fast

we write prescriptions, potent pills for your depression and the blues listing in the small-print, by the way the

drug can also lead to suicide, seizures, shaking, loss in

sex-drive, bruising, bleeding, barfing, blurry vision, racing heart and restlessness but do not worry take your

pills we'll see you in a year we wring our hands and offer

cool condolences to relatives with running noses kneel at open graves of opioid slaves their sons and daughters

fathers mothers sorry souls while seeking treatment for

their pain (not only physical in nature) crossing paths with cavalier clinicians not thinking twice doling bags of

potent pain drugs sans offering alternate ways of

treatment sentencing sufferers of pain, depression, and the plague to silent addiction without absolution

running from meeting to meeting weaving yards of red-

tape claiming it's police tape teaching spin-doctors their words in alphabetical order in any other sign language

fool the public once shame on you fool them twice

shame on them while all they did was getting sick of waiting while you sold your soul for thirty pieces and

those who could did nothing but avert the eyes wring

hands and offer cool condolences writing faster on the next prescription.

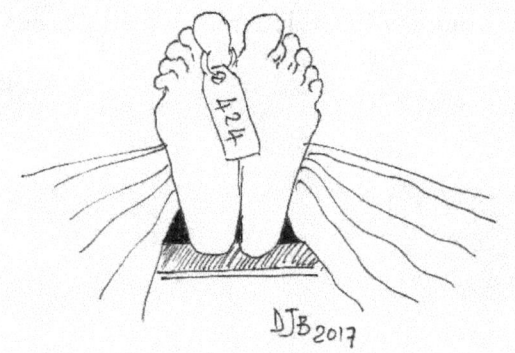

Anatomy Hall

No rumor could prepare
no terrifying tales do justice
until one stepped inside—that
first Monday morn': twelve columns
tall by eight across; shining stainless tables,
glaring gurneys, each adorned with body
wrapped in cloth—nameless numbered
mummies, embalmed; no sweet-smelling oils
and herbs, but a heady mix of equal parts of
phenol-formaldehyde—assaults the senses,
sear smelling sensibilities—injected long ago,
soon after time of death. Each and every one,
donated, their entire body, head to toe, to the
betterment of science. In hallowed reverence
we stood, gathered at the back—way back; while
herded at the front: the dean, professors, tutors,
the chirpy chaplain too; a service to be held—
in mirthless muted tones, lest we forget these
'balmed bodies once were warm-blooded men
and women, breathing souls who laughed and
leaped, danced and darted, loved and longed
and, now, lay frosted, stiff, and silent on even
colder surfaces. Their fate: subjected to
(hesitatingly unsure) dissecting knives. Lay
bare, intimate slender structures—perchance
a glimpse of footprints left among the
marrow, tendons, bones, of
the (now departed) soul.

Remedy

Remedies abound;
we've found a pill
for every pain,
(imaginary and real),
we cut, incise, excise,
each lump and bump,
nip-and-tuck, iron
wrinkles with a
knife, or shock the
catatonia from
depressive bones.
Endless sessions
on the couch, the
shrink (taking notes),
his pen chewed to pieces.
In school we learn,
exercise is medicine,
so does eating clean;
to that we've added,
writing as healing,
poetry and prose,
doing art, expression
of a thirsting soul.
And yet, (regretfully)
something's still amiss—
the bitterness that
bubbles to the surface.

Revenge can never
sooth the seething
sore—forgiveness is
what's needed: set
the bastard free, feed
him, give him water.
My God, it's hard! 'Tis
true: *He* will avenge—
the only way. *Do you
wish for healing?* No
pill but letting go.
Remedy be found.

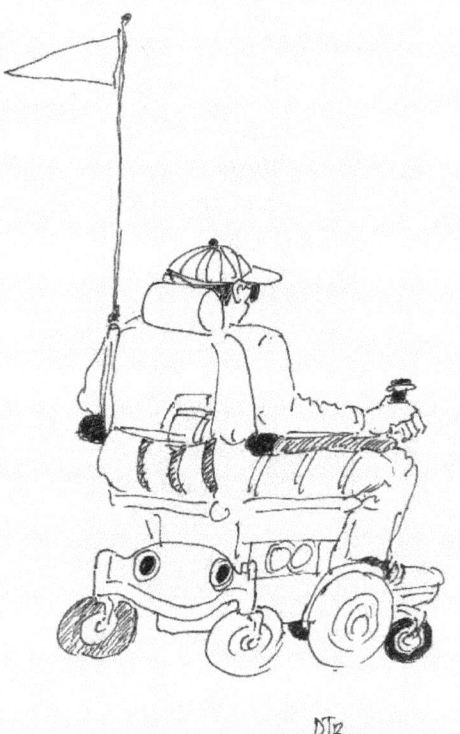

Resilience

Pedaling,

I passed a man this morning,
his dog, running on a leash,

his glance then shifted
from his four-legg'd furry friend
to meet my eye, up high,
there on the bicycle.

"Good morning!" was his greet
the radiant smile—
outdone, only
by the boist'rous wagging tail.

I watched a man this morning,
his dog, running on a leash,

with focused concentration
his shriveled hand unshaken,
maneuver wheelchair's toggle-stick.

Snow Paths

Twisting trails
through snow
through forest—
stomps uneven as if
a drunkard, as if at sea,
crunching milk-white
crystals, scaring squirrels
into hiding, making
downy woodpeckers
take flight—'till out of sight.
Rising sun paints
whiteness into shades
of iris, lilac, lavender
while knotted trunks arch
across the way, burdened
beyond breaking point,
holding hands with
brittle branches.

Lackluster stream,
frozen frigid, reflects
sky and snow and
tree for all to see
and right down
its middle, farther
back, a track,
a path—median
of the road. See?

Slither marks, the size
a snow snake makes
(Did you not know?)
Snow has turned to
flint and fossil: shades
of slate. The only
riddle to resolve—
which path to take;
make no mistake!

Part 2: Love

"My command is this:
Love each other
As I have loved you."

John 15:12 NIV

Cradle

cradle
my heart
between
calloused
hands—
lower,
lower still
below
where
the hole is
(the patch
didn't last)
fifteen
compressions
to each breath
(lock your elbows!)
hurry
hurry now
before
the sun stirs
before it
stops beating
before it
bleeds
into the sky
before you forget
the color
of my smile
before
you turn
into a pillar
of salt

Calling of a Scribe

As time turns bit-by-bit
so change the tools of trade
no less the yearning, pen an earning,
the need: be heard, share a graceful
word—ancient hands held quivering
quills, erase a smudge from dipping pen
a monstrous mess when inkwells bleed
in blue. The printing press: oh, praise the
Lord, all ignoramuses gain clues. Eighteen
eighties: scribes (once more), rejoice, as
type machines do change the game, the
need unchanged, remains the same, no
less the yearning, the need: be heard,
share a vivid word. Delightful day: birth of
brazen ballpoint pen; writing, writing,
and more writing can we do, ever faster;
little did we know, exceeded soon by
keyboard and computer, a web of internet
place whole worlds now at fingertips and
yet, the yearning ever strong—so much
noise, so many empty words. Listen, listen,
listen! we all cry louder, grab a soapbox
strong and sturdy, no, better still, grab two—
stand tall you have to rise above the din
raise your voice, you have no choice
louder still. No dammit man, you're
doing it all wrong! Perchance, if grow
silent for a day or two or three, stay

truer to my calling. Show up each
and every morn', do the solitary work,
write the words, reach out and
give and give, then rest, and know
and trust—see saplings grow, the
certain calling of a scribe

Bosom Bared

tirelessly
your wide arms
embrace
my bosom bared to an unseeing sky
your salt-kiss brush my shell-covered thighs
your white caps pounding,
pounding,
roaring,
louder than the sou'western
kissing my succulents, my sea wort, my holly
your salt-spray
snaps
shoots high
foaming, frothing,
daring, dashing,
then cry,
cry
louder than the
crestfallen call of the cormorant

Skin

lingering lips
brush butterfly
tips, pouring praises,
sweetest sweet nothings
(even a Judas kiss) elicit
a stutter, a sigh, lips parted,
while hands slide high on buttered
thigh bathed in latticed morning-
sun where longing limbs lock and
skin seek skin with yearning
that waits to hear, more than
a whispering cheer more than
a name called out with a
shudder, a shout— those
same calloused hands take
hold of hurting heart

BLACKBIRD

bobbing in the breeze,
amid cattails, the tease
conk-la-reee
do you *see?*
do you *see?*
donned in midnight-black
epaulets puffed red,
glancing, prancing
impressing ladies,
(only way to make babies)
calling, calling
conk-la-reee
glancing, prancing
head bobbing
does she see?
does she see?
answers she, in blending brown
feathers asunder, face a frown
chit, chit, chit, chit,
(no need for such a fit!)
roll of your throaty call:
a tear, bravado, a squall;
conk-la-reee
did she see?
did she see?

Love that Lingers

we long for love
that lingers, leaves
us breathless—yet
yearn more for
love in spite of,
holds us when it
hurts, or when
we stumble—
in the dark of night,
no sun in sight—
hold me, Love
that lingers

Two Figures Dancing

Her lilting love
song lags, rise
above the roaring
surf, erase fleeing footprints
paired under a crescent moon

the hunted laughs—
he's gaining, splashing through
the shallows, garments
flying—limbs and torsos luminous,
bathed in lagging lunar light

a game of love—
two figures dancing
amid the waves, her laughter dies,
drowned in consummating kisses
as lips and limbs and light align

Mended

bitterness broke
my soul in half;
turned my beating
heart to stone—
love became the
balm, grace the
yarn, that sowed
the severed shards
to one, mended what
I never could

I Should Have Loved You More

Ruthless gladiator,
hurling nets of hurts,
piercing armor (of
apparent apathy,)
as trident rips bosom-
bones apart, excises
hoping, longing, beating
heart, until no pulse remains—
when did we learn such skills?
(Both parties claim the role
of victim.) Executed with
precision: how to kill each
seed of joy, trample underfoot
a love that loved you from the
day we held you in our arms,
marveled at your tiny fists,
your fire, the dimple in your
chin. *When did it all go wrong?*
Did I ask so much: care a little
more, be a little more adult?
Our dream was never fame or
riches, (don't break your heart
in chasing it) but to be at peace,
fulfilled, live with joy and hope
amidst a world in pain and suffering,
flavored with some laughter,

an ample dose of silliness—
blessed by siblings, offspring,
friends and feisty family—
touching people's hearts
as only you can do. Perhaps
I'm not so innocent at all—
I should have loved you
more (I guess, I now
profess.) *When did
we unlearn such
solemn skills?*

Prayer Without End

against the pallid
wall,
your tapestry, prophetic now—
'the prayer without end,'
in burnt sienna, red and white

above your vacant
bed
depiction of (your long life lived)
Dutch master Maes's
oude vrouw in gebed

the intricate needle-
work;
as in the painting, so was your life:
rich in color, bordered dark,
centered light—with eternal flight

Part 3: Loss

"Grief is in two parts.
The first is loss.
The second is the
remaking of life."

Anne Roiphe

What Stays Behind

dated mattress
warm to touch—
as I labor gathering the dent
left behind
by your brittle body

at loss;
fold the pink dress
(the one you loved: did something for your skin)
clasp your hymnal
unhook the wedding picture

how to pack
a lifetime
into a faded suitcase
(without spilling tears on the content)
deciding: what stays behind

Rachel, Weeping

Weep with me.

There's a time to weep a time to laugh a time to tear robes a time to shave heads (and weep with Rachel too.) A voice sounds in Ramah*, the voice of mothers and fathers and brothers and sisters ascending the heavens.

Listen!

Hear the moaning, hear the lament for their children, lifeless mannequins, scattered between men's wear and the frozen section where Rachel, weeping for her sons and daughters, refuses to be comforted.

Weep with me.

A voice sounds in Ramah, ricocheting from El Paso to Dayton, Ohio. Shuddering, the nation grows silent, the Pharisees and leaders traipse 'round, avert the eyes, wring hands, send flowers, sing empty hallelujahs, offering heartfelt thoughts and prayers and waving flags. Hollow rhetoric their only anthem, good for stuffing turkeys, placating the public with empty promises only to do nothing, nothing but talk

O say can you see ... the land of the free?

Weep with me Rachel is weeping for her children (weep for Rachel too) only truth can set man free for if man fears, how can he be free?

O say can you see ... the home of the brave

driving out hate with hate always fail only love is stronger than fear and stronger than hate and hiding heads in the sand while flying the flag of the rifle brigade the right to bear arms while Rachel weeps for her children, lifeless mannequins, strewn asunder, waiting on the brave, men and women willing to cry out "Enough!" and help turn the tide.

Until such time, *weep with me.*

Rachel is not without hope and her wailing will (one day) turn into dancing since death came through a man (with a licensed assault rifle) and the resurrection of the dead comes through a man, the new Adam as the nation grows quiet and the Pharisees and leaders wring hands, send flowers and wave flags. Sing hopeful hallelujahs in the land of the brave. In the meantime,

weep with me

weep with the mothers and fathers and brothers and sisters and weep with Rachel too.

*With reference to Ecclesiastes 3:4; Jeremiah 31: 15 NIV

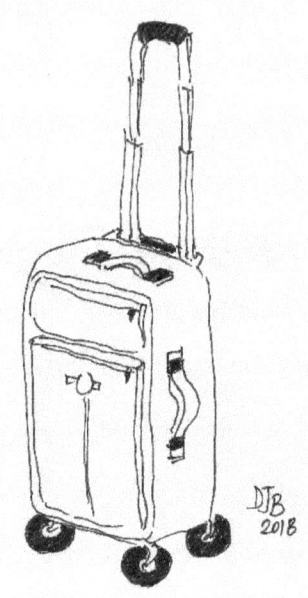

Greetings and Goodbyes

Departing years ago, set several situations in motion,
the price of which we'd pay in equal installments, distributed,
over the remnants of a long outlandish life. Off to foreign field
we'd fled; separated by an ocean, half a continent, a border
and some more—and yet, the distance merely that,
a measurement: the hand that held the phone.

Landline was the cheapest. Each time, marveled
at the cleverness of Alexander Bell, as I listened to the tender
timber in her voice, as if, standing seven steps apart. *Pappa*
also wants to speak to you, Mother always said. As I waited,
he'd shuffle closer, in slippered swollen feet,
his dancing days were over.

When are you coming back he'd croak, hopeful,
oh so hopeful, that the world he wished for, would be
like when it was when we were little and Studebakers,
shining status symbols. Each weekend I would call, and once a year,
or less, cross the sea by plane to say hello. Cramped intimately
with total strangers, shoulder touching shoulder.

Sipping tepid tea, or sweetened sugar shakes, we'd sit—
a plastic taste that lingered. Release a rental car,
slip seamlessly from lane to lane, to reach the seniors' sanctuary.
Rewarded: raw emotions rolling free, our tears,
soon would mingle—clasped her hollow hand,
the puckered skin with solar spots.

Is there a way to measure love, or loss, or longing;
a life that could have been? When bursting from her
brimming eyes, her shaking voice, her joy no match for mine.
Father joined us seven seconds later. The dozen days
we had, clutched with care to beating breasts. And that
was that. Professionals by now, of greetings and goodbyes.

THIRST

Unquenchable the thirst as my fist shake at cyan skies demanding answers for the pain the pounding the punishing standing at the bed of a man suffering, dying, who should be leaping across lilies and brooks laughing with a lover startled by the incomprehensibility of the silence to pleas and prayers and petitions and the doctor with his drugs and diagnostics shake his head measuring the grief in a father and a mother's eye as they fathom the paleness of his skin in the darkness of the moon and seven stars sweeping across the room and place a hand over my mouth and brace myself like a man and answer the questions the Lord hurled at me from the storm

while I ponder the purpose of pain and what else we can do with suffering than suffer it standing naked unable to cover my shame and my fear and my guilt with a robe or a cloak or a cloth and wonder how much I believe and the limits of faith about days cut short as a stick as I struggle to spell Leviathan and how on earth one tie his tongue with a rope or pierce his jaw with a hook and hear David sing while he walks through the valley of the shadow of death and listen to Job berating his friends for consoling him with nonsense and I hear the wild donkeys in the desert bray as the night covers my face while the church bells toll for whom the bell tolls it tolls for me what does it take to shake a man a woman a child as we live and love and lose and long and build and create and belong and it's easy to say oh forget it it's only a myth until my need is desperate and there is no other way out and I wish to see John's new Jerusalem and God himself wipe away the tears as I try to grasp the mystery of what is unseen and eternal and the resurrection of our broken brittle bodies and how we die because of Adam and how we will live because of God's son on a new earth and open a door and find a bowl filled with hope and with faith and with love (which is the greatest of the three) far outweighing my understanding and balling my

fist and shout at the sky and quenching my thirst and hiding my fear and drying my tear.

Twelve Baskets

Much easier to sit on the barren hill listening
and witness His close followers pick up twelve
baskets of left-over bread and fish and wonder
about faith and belief and the little boy than
scratching my sores and cry into the dark and
my pillow and curse the night I was born and
the day the doctor turned the monitor screen

pointing at growths in my body and the form

for the lab for the blood for the tests for the fear
and the pain in my head and my heart and my
side and my breath that caught, who, I choked,
will pick twelve baskets of me, the left-overs of
a life (lived) of a body that has so much living
left and I cannot die we will all die but I'm not
ready you'll never be ready as I pray in the garden

for this cup to pass without me drinking it as my

parched lips plead with Abraham to send Lazarus
to warn my brothers who look with indifference
at monitor screens and point out tumors to patients
with no patience and seem in no particular hurry
to heal the hurt than submit their billing and collect
their checks and go on a cruise and add a wing to
their mansion at the lake while I ponder the purpose

of pain and tear my clothes and cry to the heavens

my God, my God do not forsake me or have You
already given up on man your creations who fail
to grasp the sense of suffering while I bend down
one last time and brush my cheek against a rose
and breathe the beauty of the day as the sun
bleads into the sky and my blotched and swollen
limbs grow still and my hands lock on my love's

who rest her head on my wet cheek while the
rise and fall of my chest whistles and wanes.

HANDS

The accidental brush of hands (that first time) made you jump, fuming at my impertinence (you called it)—your indignation brightest rose, surpassed only by your parted lips. I should have walked away. Kissed you instead. The wheal of cross-cheek fingers lasted all of twenty-seven hours. *How dare you?* Spewed your lips; your eyes opposed the motion, reeled me in.

I should have walked away.

For twenty-seven days, you wouldn't take my calls or see me. When you did our hands (of their own accord) took flight, hesitant, silly, single-stringed kites, darting diamonds till you snapped the line. *Don't rush* you mouthed, your eyes however begged, *please stay*. And stayed I did. We marveled at my span of hands—covering your firm-held fists (years later, also jutting breasts); your slender fingers laced with mine, fingers trained to till the soil, hold a brush, adjust a microphone, suckle child without a blush, make music with a flute, be lover—'twas a hoot!

Should I have walked away?

For twenty-seven years you woke me with those hands, cupped my face, kissed my eyes and ears and lips—prostrated front to front, breast to breast, laced fingers, limbs and loins. A love that buoyed and bound and healed and drowned all pain. Until one day, your fingers found a lump that stayed—denial first—'twas so futile. And thus, began our fretful journey. Your loving fingers, used to lace with mine, white-knuckled on examination tables, while foreign fingers (cold to touch) palpated, probed and poked—forgetting to inquire how you felt.

I could never walk away. Rest your hand, here, on my cheek.

For twenty-seven weeks they tested, trialed, tomographed—as long it took the tumor to get rated, while we, for all, but waited. Now, our laced-together hands seek merely certainty. Serenity. Scalpels circumcised your wounded chest, cut away your breathless breasts, (you wept, I mourned my little friends.) In synchrony, poison poured through ports from plastic bags, killing uninvited guests as well as haze the host. We prayed, believed and hoped on healing. If no cure, we'd settle for remission. How brave is those who bargain. Brazen. Bold. *O, God!*

Rest your hand here on my cheek—one more time

A second twenty-seven weeks was all it needed, wring the life 'twas left from you. And yet, you never ceased to reach, cup my face and rest your hand on either cheek. Each accidental brush (like the first time) made me jump, clasping moments, memories, repeat your name. Unspoken longing, words our lips not dared, our eyes would speak, and sing. You warned me it was time, your hands much cooler, unable for a final reach. Lacing fingers, I leaned closer. My love. My Love. *I love you* mouthed your parted lips. Your soul already soaring.

Rest your hand here on my cheek—one last time

Footpaths

(Translated from Afrikaans: *Voetpadlangs*)

Barefoot, my heart fled
along the footpath up the
mountain to where the earth
dropped away and the mist
wrapped me in its arms—an
alabaster veil, no beginning and no
end—wordless, with no ill will: day
turned night: the whitest night

Countless the little paths we
have wandered together. When
you were young, I carried you, trying
to answer your thousand-and-one
questions. Bush paths, mountain
paths, from where we viewed the
endless valleys, where you, in later
years, would bare your soul

Rock paths, where we had to dig
stones from our boots. Your
laughter—how my empty heart
yearns for that silliness. Coastal paths,
from where the ochre sphere of a
morning sun inched out above the sea,
and half a day further, we'd bade the
glowing globe of red farewell

The beach paths where our footprints
were casted in wet sand, and came
evening, on the way back, the tide
had washed the slate clean. Your desire
for shells so limitless—one the size of
a child's fist—tight against the ear:
the sea, do you hear? A gull's lament,
wafting, interwoven with the waves

Call of a Cormorant, perched upon the pier,
wings spread, in customary benediction.
With hollow hands my heart keeps
record of the yesterdays—all treasures—
an impossible task: wrap each day in the
finest tissue paper, cherished against my
cheek, where my heart beats, feel it beat.
Beat. Beat. Will I face defeat?

My heart is mute. No more dispute.
Surrounded in silence—merciful silence.
In my chest the pomegranate bursts red,
smothering my cries, my incessant weeping.
Naked I entered the world. And naked . . .
The Lord took. Throughout the night,
with an angel I wrestled till daybreak.
I won't let go unless You bless me.

Barefoot, my heart fled
along the footpath up the
mountain to where the earth
dropped away and the mist
wrapped me in its arms—wordless,
with no ill will: the whitest night

Come early morning, a balmy
breeze sweeps from the sea, tears
stifling mist apart—right next to
me I see, an unknown footpath leading
from the hill. My heart, now cautious,
shuffles down the narrow path.

Voetpadlangs

(Along footpaths—see English translation: Footpaths # 27)

*Kaalvoet vlug my hart
met die voetpad teen die
berg uit tot waar die aarde
wegval en die mis sy arms
uitsteek—my omhels met 'n
waas sonder begin of einde—
verwytloos, woordeloos; waar
dag nag word: die witste nag.*

*Ontelbaar die paadjies wat
ons saam gestap het. In die begin,
toe jy klein was, moes ek jou dra,
en poog om jou duisend-en-een vrae
te beantwoord. Bospaadjies,
bergpaadjies, vanwaar ons valleie
en dale kon aanskou, waar jy,
later jare, jou hart kon ontbloot.*

*Klip paadjies, waar ons klippe uit
ons stewels moes grawe. Jou lag—
my leë hart hunker na jou lawwe lag.
Kuspaadjies, vanwaar ons die more-
son se oker bal agter die see
sien uitkruip het, en 'n halwe dag
verder, agter dieselfde oseaan, die
gloeiende bol rooi vaarwel kon toeroep.*

Die strand paadjies waar ons twee rye
voetpore in nat sand gegiet is, en teen
die aand se kant, met ons terugkeer, die
gety ons spore met sorg glad gewas het. Jou
behoefde aan 'n skulp was grensloos—die
grootte van 'n kind se vuis—styf teen die oor:
hoor die see se geruis! Meeu se weeklaag,
sweef, ineen geweef met rustelose waters.

Kormorant, kordaat op 'n verweerde kaai,
vleuels uitgesprei—'n predikant wat seën.
Met hande bak , hou my hart notule
van al die gisters—kostelike skatte—
'n onmoontlike taak: vou elke dag in
fynste sneespapier, koester teen my
wang, waar my hart nog klop. Voel dit
klop. Klop. Klop. Wanneer sal dit stop?
My hart is stom. My lippe krom. Gehul
in stilte—genadige stilte. In my bors
bars die granaat rooi; smoor my kras
krete, my geweeklag—naak het ek
in die wêreld gekom. En naak . . .
Die Here het geneem. In die nanag
worstel ek met 'n engel tot dagbreek.
Ek sal nie laat los todat U my seën.

Kaalvoet vlug my hart
met die voetpad teen die
berg uit tot waar die aarde
wegval en die mis sy arms
uitsteek—my omhels—verwyt-
loos, woordeloos; die witste nag.

*Teen die vroeë môre, pluk 'n
warm wind van die kaai se kant
die wasigheid aan flarde—neffens
my lei 'n onbekende voetpad teen
die berg af. My hart, versigtig, met bak
hande, skuifel met die voetpad langs.*

In Memoriam: Father

Unfathomable our failure
measuring the temperament of time,
the shallow shelf life of our pain,
the color of a life once lived,
fractured as it was.
His love: (calculate the lack thereof)
Adds up, scorned and spurned—
unwilling to absolve.
Two dozen lunar cycles hence—
a locust plague preferred;
senseless, heartless, almost homeless,
fail to shelve his truckload blemishes.
Noble notion it is not,
nor raising flags in white,
but healing of the self;
unlock all manacles,
acquit the dead, set free.
Take hands—brothers,
sisters, mine.

Measuring a Life

Tired eyes,
ringed in sunless
shadows, fluttered
at the breeze—my
arrival in her room.
Recognition registering
in her grasp, rasping
words wobbled past
parched lips, *You've
come. Too late*, echoes
accusingly across ages
as sand sifts through a
narrow neck, measuring
time, measuring a life.
Immeasurable. I wrap
her wrinkles together
with her laughter, her
lingering love, unspoken
words, and hurts hurled
at her through the years.
Her hollow hands,
sunspot-speckled
cooling down—the
once formidable
flame flickers, the
initial burst and
whoosh of fireworks
sputters.

Cradling
her wilted frame,
ear at her lips
capturing waning
whispers—*love* . . .
she lisps, *tell the
others . . . you
must love* . . .

Part 4: Longing

"The best and most
beautiful things in the world
cannot be seen
or even touched—
they must be felt in the heart."

Helen Keller

Wonder

hold your breath
and ponder—
the sound
the sun makes
on its way to rest,
the bursting
brimming
choruses—
as pastels paint
the skies and trees
and seas

May You

may the wind kiss your
skin again, may you
follow a bird in flight,
seek a friend to hug,
embrace a cup of tea,
warm your heart with
loud and silly laughter,
feel the touch of hands,
marvel at intricate
flowers—may the wind
kiss your skin again

Cormorant

wide and white the sand,
rocks, black and bothered,
taking on the shape of water—
drums against the ribcage of the
shore, beats, caresses, sweep its
mighty arms, cleanse—in bravest
cobalt-blues, liquid light with salt—
preserving, frothing, foaming—
hands cupped, catch the cry
of cormorant—framed by
solemn cyan skies

Be Still

astounding, endless, the
cunning and the cleverness,
the masks my troubled
heart parades; master of
charades . . . search me,
search my troubled, tangled
mind . . . the burden of my
tumbling, stumbling thoughts;
be still my stricken soul,
be quiet (for a change);
my God, how vast your
heavens, illimitable
your searing thoughts;
be still my soul
be still!

Last Week's Embrace

Wandering through
empty rooms—hollow
steps, listening to
yesterday's laughter,
reaching . . . for last
week's embrace

Brother

sorrow seven-fold
on bitterness a hold
your empty place
I daily face,
brother mine—
my hollow hands
scoop manna
in the morning,
mercy (all unmerited.)
accept my cloak:
forgiveness forged
from tears and loss
and longing—goodness
not my own—merely
granted grace.
brother mine
resume your place?

Enough

Today:
will I
be enough?
Will I
go unnoticed?
Will you
hear my
silent cry,
see the sliver
of my soul?

No Slaves to Yesterdays

Impossible as it is to stop the sun's
red nail rise behind the sea—so light outruns

the desperation (like a birthright) with which
we cling and pull a blanket tight—hide the snitch,

at fault, keeping darkness in. Our seagull's screech
washes wider than the far horizon's reach,

shouting shameless accusations. Heavens help!
My God, 'tis so much to ask—absolve that whelp?

Seemingly untired centuries-old waves
wash beaches white at night—squalor waived; no slaves

to yesterdays, leave behind a debris-line:
a virgin slate reflects—the sky, sun, align

Seven times stubborner than braying donkeys,
scoop rubble, instead of shells, sea stars; *montes*,

if not mountains we've molded, in our hunger—
hold to hurt, time and date offense—hatemonger

we've become (by choice), wardens of personal
prisons, shackled to the past—what a pickle

we've created, (again by choice), ruminate
the wrongs, cherish chewing bile; it is not fate.

Only way to beach your boat is row—easy,
sinks the ship, grant mercy—abandon seedy

Impossible as it is to stop the sun's
silent cycle, hoarding hate hurts health, dear ones

Eyes to the sky, hear the fish eagle cry, call
of the cormorant—forgive—be free—'tis all!

I Will Rise

Brimming with scorn
the lady stooped low,
severed the fragrant
flower with stem
crushed it completely.
"Oh, but she's blind!" the little girl cried

I will rise
to the skies

Shaking with haste
the hunter hacked harder
ripped the heart beating from
the dear's chest, paying no heed
to the bleats and the grunts
"Oh, but he's deaf!" the little boy cried

I will rise
no more cries

Frothing with fervor
the centurion heated
the iron seven times seven
poked out both eyes
of the girl who would think
"Oh, he's a coward!" the little girl cried

I will rise
more goodbyes

Cackling with glee
the captain slammed boards
with holes for the hands
and one for the head; locked the man
down. The hapless one's crime:
"He used the word *ethics*," the little boy cried

I will rise
I have worth

Each morning at dusk
when roosters crow loud—
people would gather and laugh,
point at the stocks and spit at his face
like vultures above
"He's a rotten tomato," the little girl cried

I will rise
I am loved

How close to a lie
a truth that is twisted
formidable fables concocted
then dished up as gospel, as leaders,
warped in deceit, avert all their eyes
"Innocent—burnt at the stakes!" the little boy cried

I will rise
I'll not hate

I will rise
I found grace

I will rise
I found hope

I will rise
I have wings
I will rise

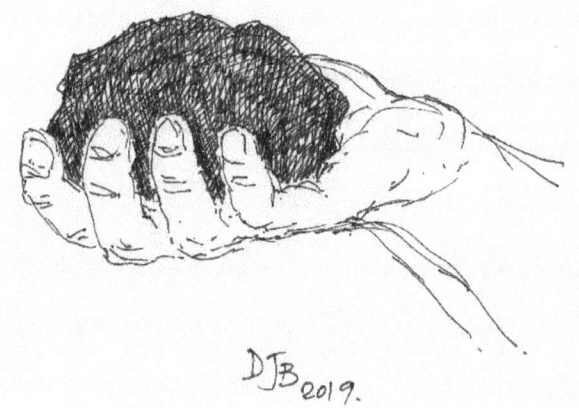

WHAT'S IN YOUR HAND?

Murmurs ripple through the crowd
the throng, the pushing, shoving mass,
each cradling rocks, the size of fists, hands hidden;
their instigators holding back—dressed in their finest, robed
in red—reiterating, nodding as on cue: *the law commands…*

They drag and shove the hapless figure forward
cast her to the street of dirt, bruised and halfway broken
hands behind her back with plastic ties (buy them at the corner
-hardware store) pointing fingers—**Teacher, she's so bad*, their voices
break, drop to a whisper: *Can you believe what she's done? The law commands…*

The teacher kneels, and writes there in the sand
ignores the furor, their spitting anger; using fingers, with his hand
the leader stomps his staff, repeats the charge, *Teacher, this woman…*
I know the accusations—the Man looks up from where he writes—*let those without fault be first to fling a stone.* He bends down and writes some more

Then, when silence closes in on them, the teacher seeks the woman's eyes her sobs now silent, her whimpering wanes, she struggles to her feet, the street entirely empty. *No executioners? Not one who wishes see you hang? Not one,* she says. The teacher cuts her free: *Neither do I. Go. Do what's right.*

What's in *your* hand? A hand-held mirror or a savage stone?

*John 8: 3-11 NIV

Part 5: Laughter & Joy

"While suffering is inevitable,
misery is optional.
Pain cannot be avoided,
but joy can.
If you don't believe
in the power of choice,
you won't experience it."

Mike Mason

Two Bowls of Joy

first thing after sunrise,
scoop two bowls of joy—
manna from the desert floor;
one you soak your heart in,
the other pour it out: on friend
and foe and foreigner—
the only, only, way
for peace to stay

Joy Comes in the Morning

set aside your sadness
close your book of wrongs
from the basket at the door
choose gladness, pick joy up
from the floor amidst the
sorrow and the strife,
(even living an ordinary life)
seek gratitude, content
with what we have—find
joy in simple things:
the whisper of the wind
the brush of loving hands
a tablespoon of moon
laughter with a friend
the aromatic rouge of roses—
a joy that lives and cannot die

Silly Poem

On Fridays write a silly poem
with rhythm, rhymes with gastronome

for fizzy friends and family
for readers with a cup of tea

for fun, for lovers of rare words,
then write, divide the page in thirds

ten silly things: read with a hat
eat with a knife, kiss a fat cat

blow through a straw, sing on the train
sleep in the church, dance in the rain

walk on your hands, sit in a tree
laugh every day, your soul'll be free

on Fridays write a silly poem
with rhythm, rhymes with metronome

Slice of Sun

Here, may I
sit beside you?
(I'll shut up,
I promise.)
I'll hold your
hand—thaw the
hoar frost in
your heart—
may I open
a shutter?
(the attic
one will do)
let in a slice
of sun—and,
for a moment,
still your sorrow,
sooth your sore—
may I?

Traffic Light Troubadour

No crudely concocted
cardboard cry for help
(in usual sooted scribble)—
Please help: No food,
No family, No fare.
Instead, head thrown
back, strumming a
seasoned six-string—
sun-bleached as his mane—
eyes on unseen mountains,
a beat-up boot tapping tune,
faithful at his only piece of
real estate, his trusted traffic light.

A voice that carries—above
the thrum of trucks and trailers,
in former life a tenor in a choir!
As light turns red, drivers forced
to linger, listen to the minstrel's
song—no plead for pity, refusal
to feel shame, his lucid eyes a
dare: meet my gaze you blessed
of man and beast, cocooned
in air-conditioned Cadillacs.
Save your scorn. *Spare change?*
Tonight, we'll feast. Perchance to
dine and dream and dare.

Beach Day (at the Lake)

Half the joy lay
nestled (in the
planning), packing
of provisions; buns
and butter, ham and
cheese with holes,
cucumber slices,
bottled water, and
soda in a can, chilled,
huddled in a cooler.
Incessant chatter of the
grandkids, effervescent,
lotioned, sandalled, each
buttressed in broad-rimmed
hats. Checkered tablecloth,
red and white, six clips to hold
it tight, prevent the plastic
taking flight. Folding chairs in
bags, stuffed and strapped—
red wagon pulled behind.

Early morning hour offers early
bird the worm, staking claim:
prime real estate, a cherished
spot with trees, a patch of grass,
full view of a khaki-colored beach,
turquoise water lapping, licking
yesterday's sandcastles, structured
in a C. No peace be had, yank
T-shirts, dress went flying, "Come
Oupa!" the collective call, "And *Ouma*
too!" She laughs and waves them
on, youthful stampeders racing
through the waves. Splashing for
two hours, small enough to still
wear floating things, (in delightful
neon colors.) Lips turned blue
and fingers into raisins—time
for tea and towels. At last a sun,
burst from hiding, bathe clad
and semi-clad with golden gloss.

Umbrellas—colors of the
rainbow snap and zing, jangle
in the breeze scattered, 'cross
the sand where ladies in bikinis,
bronze limbs and partial-covered
breasts, lounge and sigh on towels,
rubbing lotion, endless motion,
enough to mirror clouds. Seven
men, a single lass, spike ball
across a net, diving sideways,
spitting sand. A day with sun and
sand and sunscreen beg for ice
cream in a cone, a scoop of mint,
(or choc'late), "please, can I have two?"
Her little hands drenched in melting
taste of heaven, lips and chin a mess,
unable to hold stable, the sliding precipice,
plops to the thirsty sand. Cheeks all wet,
a gull cries overhead—time to wrap
it up and greet the dazzling day.

Morning

yesterday's shackles
jingle
on wet sand
leaving man-on-the-moon
footprints

ocean's breath inhale
embrace her restless pulse
slant eyes against
a rising sun
step wide—a jelly fish!

clean slate:
(a virgin beach) each morn'
along the debris-line
screech gulls, a cormorant
make manacles fall wide

To Joy be Drawn

Unwilling does the forest, uncross her arms
at dawn. Permit the first fair light, stray
slithers spill upon the swerving way, charms
early wand'rers with brittle birth of day

between the legs of giants, dance phantoms
white, twirl from the forest floor—shapeless
apparitions—darkness flees in quantums;
burnt sienna, greens, prairie rose caress

the mindful eye; revive inquisitive
observers as they amble on their way.
Startled, prance the white-tailed fawn all festive,
with spotted coat, across the path away

scant price it is to pay, rise early, make
headway on the sun—before its heav'nly arch.
Enfold by trees—the gift is yours to take:
blessings to unwrap, tranquil is the march

speak sparse, be cognizant, awareness is
your tool, the wildwood seldom suffers fools:
brass guest, creatures of the bush, when displease—
will hide or flee, deny a glimpse: the rules

uncommon it is not, benediction
to receive, when humble stride at dawn
touch her heartbeat, breath her scent, devotion
to the forest; uplift, to joy be drawn

Moonlit Beaches

traipse with me across
pallid, moonlit beaches—
arm-in-arm with frothing
foam, we'll dance to
drumbeat of the blue—
our laughter darting,
dashing: birds in flight;
we'll braid the tails of
seven stars as crowns

Gift

Received a gift this early morn':
a day with four and twenty hours,
wrapped in diaphanous rays,
bounty of bright colors,
imbued, aroma-filled:
hope and second chances—
I cried, then laughed,
and stepped into the sun.

THANK YOU FOR READING!

If you loved this collection of poems, please tell a family member, a neighbor, or a friend! Don't be afraid to share!

We all live complex and colorful lives. We all experience pain and struggle and sorrow—however, each day, our option remains: misery or joy? It is my sincere wish and hope that you may discover and taste the liberating power of joy, however difficult life may be, realizing, that it remains to a large extent, a choice.

A bowl of joy to you!

Please consider leaving an *online review*. Reviews matter. By leaving a review (on Amazon) more readers will gain access to the collection of poems and novels and enable the author to write more.

Also by Danie Botha

1. *Be Silent*
2. *Be Good*
3. *Maxime*
4. *Young Maxime*
5. *An Unfamiliar Kindness*

Find more of my writing at
https://daniebotha.com

www.ingramcontent.com/pod-product-compliance
Lightning Source LLC
Chambersburg PA
CBHW070524100426
42743CB00010B/1946